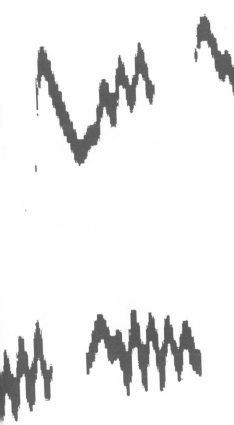

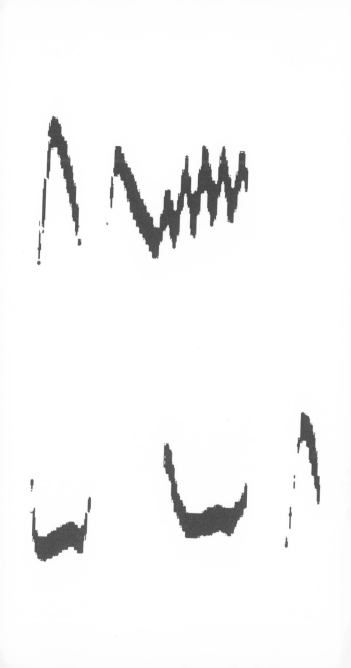

Aaaaw to Zzzzzd

The Words of Birds

Aaaaw to Zzzzzd

The Words of Birds

North America, Britain, and Northern Europe

John Bevis
with photographs by the author

THE MIT PRESS   CAMBRIDGE, MASSACHUSETTS   LONDON, ENGLAND

MIT Press books may be purchased at special quantity discounts for business or sales promotional use. For information, please email special_sales@mitpress.mit.edu or write to Special Sales Department, The MIT Press, 55 Hayward Street, Cambridge, MA 02142.

This book was set in Minion and Scala Sans by Graphic Composition, Inc. Printed and bound in Canada.

Library of Congress Cataloging-in-Publication Data

Bevis, John, 1954–

Aaaaw to zzzzzd : the words of birds : North America, Britain, and northern Europe / John Bevis ; with photographs by the author

p. cm.

Includes bibliographical references.

ISBN 978-0-262-01429-8 (hardcover : alk. paper)

1. Birdsongs—North America—Identification. 2. Birdsongs—Europe, Northern—Identification. 3. Sounds, Words for. I. Title. II. Title : Words of birds.

QL698.5.B48 2010

598.159′4—dc22

2009045904

10 9 8 7 6 5 4 3 2 1

1. The same signal may be used for different things, and different signals for the same thing.

2. The sounds produced by no two species are exactly alike.

Acknowledgments

This book originated with a simple whim: to make a list of words used to notate birdsong. The result was, and would have remained, a bundle of file cards, had it not been for Simon Cutts. Poet, publisher, gallerist, and pivotal figure in artists' books internationally, Simon saw the ways and means of turning my woolly notion into book form. *An A-Z of Bird Song*, which combined a lexicon for the birds of Britain with some found photos whose captions were intended to disarm, appeared in 1995 as a joint publication of Simon's Coracle Press and Greville Worthington's St Paulinus Press. Colin Sackett, himself a book artist of repute, designed and saw it through production.

To my bemusement the book was well received and eventually sold out. One copy made its way, through the mutual acquaintance of the late Jonathan Williams, poet, publisher, and truffle hound of Anglo-American subculture, into the hands of Roger Conover, who is not only Executive Editor at the MIT Press but yet another poet-editor-originator of books. In the course of subsequent discussions between Simon and Roger over potential joint projects, the feasibility of a second edition of *An A-Z of Bird Song* arose.

Something about the idea must have clicked with Roger, as he and I were soon in email contact, by which I mean I was shortly in an intriguing debate fired by his suggestions, inspiration, and enthusiasm. Roger took the decision to turn this into an MIT Press publication, and suggested I expand it to its present scope and form.

Roger Conover has done so much in visualizing and nurturing this project that his name should appear on the title page alongside mine. Also at MIT, Anar Badalov has fielded forms and instructions with great humor, tact, and patience. Matthew Abbate, manuscript editor, has Americanized my original English, checked the accuracy of my facts and the consistency of their presentation, and made many elegant improvements to my prose. Designer Erin Hasley has turned my vague notion of the book looking "something like a pocketbook" into an object of style.

I would like to thank Simon Cutts and Colin Sackett, not only for the original *An A-Z of Bird Song* but also for their encouragement and advice over many years; Les Coleman and Harry Gilonis for the resources they generously put my way; Alec Connah for sharing his bird wisdom; and Linda, who has been endlessly supportive.

In memory of my father Derek Bevis, 1923–2008.

5. Each species may sing differently from place to place.

6. No two individual birds sing exactly alike.

Meredith suggested the lark could: "The song seraphically free / Of taint of personality"?[14]

We are aware that the art we make is a premeditated confection, whose integrity we fear may be compromised by value judgments and commodity status. No such problem for birdsong. Meredith, again, captured our sense of the rightness of birdsong, its lack of affectation, its inevitable sequence: "So rich our human pleasure ripes / When sweetness on sincereness pipes." And it is not difficult to think of more than one way in which "We want the key of his wild note, / Of truthful in a tuneful throat."

Art is a mystery to us, though we devote libraries and institutions to decoding it, supposing that what man may make mystery, man may make rational. But birdsong will remain, as Robert Bridges wrote in "Nightingales," the "dark nocturnal secret."[15] Similarly Thomas Hardy finds an enigmatic intelligence in "The Darkling Thrush": "That I could think there trembled through / His happy good-night air / Some blessed Hope, whereof he knew / And I was unaware."[16]

So birdsong is, like other arts, truth in rehearsal. More than other arts it is incorruptible, vital, sublime. The ultimate claim, which might be the aspiration of any man-made art, is found in "March the Third" by Edward Thomas: "The birds' songs have / The holiness gone from the bells,"[17] or again in "Merlin's Song," where Ralph Waldo Emerson suggests "In the heart of the music peals a strain / Which only angels hear."[18] It is our ecstasy, our resolve, our frustration, to realize ourselves on the brink of hearing that strain.

7. Each bird may sing differently from time to time.

8. A song may be repetitious and monotonous, or it may be random and unpredictable.

Garstang that "by a rhythmic syllabic notation alone it is possible to imitate the dominant features of a song closely enough to be distinctive and recognizable."[23]

The period of greatest coinage of bird words came when birdwatching was a burgeoning hobby, with an attendant demand for field guides, before sound recording. A verbal code such as that suggested by Walter Garstang, legible, quantifiable, and improvable, offered the best approximation to the ideal of fixing and standardizing a record of the way we hear birdsong. But where we might have expected harmony, there was discord. Like birds practicing for the best possible rendition, naturalists have improvised and improved on their own and each other's results, occasionally agreeing, sometimes quite at odds, but most often rendering the same sound in variations that are nitpickingly slight. So we do not have a standardized *jug* or a *tereu* for all, or even more than a few, of the birds; the lexicon included in this book is offered as evidence toward a debate as to whether we should.

9. There is a wide variety in the purity and character of the notes.

10. The more highly developed the song, the greater the range of variation.

Introduction to the Lexicon

What follows is an attempt to compile the most plausible notations for the most distinctive calls of the most commonly heard birds of North America, Britain, and northern Europe.

That geographical coverage relates to the distribution of this book more than the distribution of birds. In fact, looking through distribution charts it strikes me that the short-eared owl is possibly the only species (other than booksellers) to breed exclusively where this book is sold. For the rest, the charts show no two species occupying precisely the same territories for residing, breeding, wintering, and visiting on passage.

The overall picture then is daunting, but fortunately for us population distributions are far from haphazard. Geographical divides—oceans and mountains—restrict the range of the majority, particularly the arboreal birds. The idea that this may have resulted in more or less permanent territorial groupings of species was first proposed in "Some Difficulties in Zoological Distribution" by the English zoologist Philip L. Sclater in 1878.[25] He argued that the world population of birds inhabits six discrete regions, roughly allied to the principal land masses, and each with its own substantially exclusive avifauna. North America lies within the Nearctic region, Britain and northern Europe within the Palearctic.

The list of "regular" species for that part of the Nearctic covered by this book numbers a little over eight hundred, and for the equivalent zone of the Palearctic something less than five hundred. There is, though, a significant crossover between these two particular regions, especially among aquatic species, birds of prey, owls (of course), and a potpourri of passerines, notably various finches. The numbers are bolstered by introduced species, such as the house sparrow and starling in North America and the parakeet in Britain. In all about 120 species are resident in both areas; a further twenty-odd Palearctic species occasionally occur in America, while fifty Nearctic types are irregular visitors to Europe. More commonality is indicated by eighty or so species in the one zone being represented by almost identical forms in the other. These junctures led T. H. Huxley to recommend that the two regions should be considered allied subregions.

The purposes of the book, whether as field guide or lexical curiosity, seem best served by listing the two regions separately here. Common species are included on both lists, but the notations of their calls are original to the zones in which they appear, so that the tree creeper in the one list may be ascribed a different notation than the identical brown creeper in the other. Perverse this may seem, but like wine birdsong does not always travel well, and *Certhia familiaris* may be sweeter there than here.

Some eligible species not included in the lists are the rare visitors, those with very small and local populations, and those with no distinct voice. The birds marked down as "generally silent" include a few of the larger raptors and many aquatic species, including examples of petrels, shearwaters, cormorants, gannets, boobies, skuas, auklets, puffins, and some ducks.

Of the species common to both zones, some share common English-language names, or slight variations ("starling" and "European starling"; "eider" and "common eider"). For those that do not, the equivalent British and American names are shown here, the British on the left.

great northern diver	common loon
black-throated diver	arctic loon
red-throated diver	red-throated loon
black-necked grebe	eared grebe
Slavonian grebe	horned grebe
cormorant	great cormorant
great white egret	common egret
night heron	black-crowned night heron
teal	green-winged teal
wigeon	European wigeon
scaup	greater scaup
long-tailed duck	oldsquaw
eider	common eider
velvet scoter	white-winged scoter
goosander	common merganser
brent goose	brant
Bewick's swan	whistling swan
rough-legged buzzard	rough-legged hawk
hen harrier	marsh hawk
merlin	pigeon hawk
willow grouse	willow ptarmigan
ptarmigan	rock ptarmigan
rock partridge	chukar
partridge	gray partridge
pheasant	ring-necked pheasant
moorhen	common gallinule
oystercatcher	American oystercatcher
turnstone	ruddy turnstone
Kentish plover	snowy plover
grey plover	black-bellied plover
snipe	common snipe
common sandpiper	spotted sandpiper

black-winged stilt	black-necked stilt
grey phalarope	red phalarope
red-necked phalarope	northern phalarope
arctic skua	parasitic jaeger
pomarine skua	pomarine jaeger
long-tailed skua	long-tailed jaeger
great skua	skua
common gull	mew gull
kittiwake	black-legged kittiwake
little tern	least tern
puffin	common puffin
guillemot	common murre
Tengmalm's owl	boreal owl
three-toed woodpecker	northern three-toed woodpecker
shore lark	horned lark
swallow	barn swallow
sand martin	bank swallow
blue-headed wagtail	yellow wagtail
waxwing	Bohemian waxwing
great grey shrike	northern shrike
wren	winter wren
tree creeper	brown creeper
Lapland bunting	Lapland longspur
redpoll	common redpoll
crossbill	red crossbill
two-barred crossbill	white-winged crossbill
magpie	black-billed magpie
raven	common raven

13. Some species sing only in the mating season, others all year round.

14. Some species mimic the voices of other species.

Lexicon for North America

aaaaw   black skimmer

aaayayaum   Caspian tern

aach   gull-billed tern

aan aan aan aan aan aan   mangrove cuckoo

ah-ah-ah-ah   common merganser

ank ank ank   red-breasted nuthatch

aou aou   ring-billed gull

arrr arrr   Barrow's goldeneye, common goldeneye

bee-bz-bz-bz   golden-winged warbler

beee-bzzz   blue-winged warbler

beep   least grebe

beesh   scaled quail

beet   canyon wren

bek   gadwall

bek bek bek   red-throated loon

bink   bobolink, golden-crowned sparrow

bit bit bit   brown-headed nuthatch

bob-white   northern bobwhite

brek   cattle egret

brooo brooo brooo   snowy owl

broooo broooo broooo king eider

brreet willow flycatcher

brrrrrr Carolina wren

br-r-r-rt dicksissel

brrr-zee thick-billed kingbird

brrt bank swallow

bup-bup bup-bup-bup king rail

bzeep American woodcock

bzzz golden-cheeked warbler

cac-cac-cac sharp-tailed grouse

cah fish crow

caw American crow

caw-caw-caw-caw-coodle-yah American crow

cha cha cha clapper rail

cha cha cha cha cha cactus wren

cha-cha-lac plain chachalaca

ch-ack ringed kingfisher

chack bluethroat, Brewer's blackbird, common grackle, long-billed thrasher

chack-weet weet-chack northern wheatear

chap ovenbird

chap chap chap chap chap sedge wren

charr gray vireo

ch-ch-ch-ch black-tailed gnatcatcher

chchchchchchchchch Wilson's warbler

che-bek least flycatcher

che-bunk yellow-bellied flycatcher

che-che-che-che European starling

check dicksissel, house wren, northern mockingbird

check check check Wilson's phalarope

chee chee Bell's vireo

cheedle cheedle cheedle water pipit

cheeeeev red-tailed hawk

cheeeh black-tailed gnatcatcher

cheek Harris's sparrow

chee-lick buff-breasted flycatcher

cheepit, chuwee, cheepit, psee dusky flycatcher

cheereek osprey

cheerily cheer-up cheerio American robin

cheery cheery cheery Carolina wren

cheet tree swallow

cheeva cheeva cheeva tufted titmouse

cheezp dunlin

che-ik ee-ik ee-ik Anna's hummingbird

chekar scaled quail

chep common yellowthroat

cherr purple martin

chertee-chertee-chertee ovenbird

chet chet chet whew whew hooded oriole

chew purple martin

chewidee cheedle chew Bell's vireo

chewink eastern towhee, rufous-sided towhee

chewip gray flycatcher

chi-bew Cassin's kingbird

chi-ca-go California quail

chi-ca-go-go Gambel's quail

chick Anna's hummingbird, downy woodpecker, five-striped sparrow, rufous-capped warbler, white-eyed vireo, white-headed woodpecker

chick-adee-adee-adee mountain chickadee

chick-a-dee-dee bridled titmouse

chick-a-dee-dee-dee black-capped chickadee, Carolina chickadee

chicky-tucky-tuck summer tanager

chiddik chiddik house sparrow

chiddle-chiddle-chiddle turtle MacGillivray's warbler

chi-deery crissal thrasher

chidi-ew painted redstart

chidp chestnut-sided warbler

chif chif chif hoary redpoll

chik bereek groove-billed ani

chik-chik chik-chik northern shoveler

chikikikikikikikikik ladder-backed woodpecker

chimp black-and-white warbler

chimp chimp winter wren

chinga chinga chinga swamp sparrow

chinginginginging arctic warbler

chink blue grosbeak, brown towhee, green-tailed towhee, Nashville warbler, Virginia's warbler, white-throated sparrow

chink tree tree tree Louisiana waterthrush

chip Bewick's wren, Botteri's sparrow, Cassin's sparrow, chipping sparrow, eastern phoebe, Grace's warbler, lucifer hummingbird, magnificent hummingbird, orange-crowned warbler, sedge wren, verdin, vesper sparrow, violet-green swallow, yellow warbler

chip-a chip-a chip-a common snipe

chip-burr scarlet tanager

chip chillip black-whiskered vireo

chip-chip-chip pine warbler

chip chip wheedle wheedle che yellow-eyed junco

chip-chup-ee chip-chup-ee Connecticut warbler

chir-ee-eep least tern

chirp evening grosbeak, house sparrow

chirrip royal tern

chit boreal chickadee

chit-ah black-capped vireo

chit chit chit towee common redpoll

chit-chit-chit weet weet violet-green swallow

chit-ee-up chit-ee-up Cassin's finch

chiup brown towhee

chi-weep roseate tern

chk-chk-chk wood thrush

chlee-ip pine siskin

chlip-chlip-chlip-chlip-wuk-wuk Virginia's warbler

chok Kentucky warbler

ch-ree ch-ree ch-ree Kentucky warbler

ch-reee ch-reee ch-reee rock wren

chrrr-chrrr-chrrr Bonaparte's gull

chtttr long-billed thrasher

chuck Bendire's thrasher, black-billed magpie, bronzed cowbird, brown thrasher, brown-headed cowbird, California thrasher, hepatic tanager, orchard oriole, sage thrasher, seaside sparrow, yellow-rumped warbler

chuck-ar chuck-ar chuck-ar chukar

chuck chuck hermit thrush

chuck chuck chuck gray jay

chug lark bunting, red-bellied woodpecker, red-headed woodpecker

chuif magnolia warbler

chuk bobolink, great-tailed grackle

chu-leet American golden plover

chup varied thrush

chup chup chup spotted towhee

chup-chup-tzee seaside sparrow

chupp Canada warbler

chur chur-lee chur-lee eastern bluebird

churk pectoral sandpiper, semipalmated plover, semipalmated sandpiper

churp elf owl

churr brown thrasher, Cassin's kingbird, cliff swallow, Gila woodpecker, mountain bluebird, red-bellied woodpecker, sage thrasher

churr-churr golden-fronted woodpecker

churr churr shurr red-bellied woodpecker

chu-wee cheerio solitary vireo

chu-wee chu-weet gray vireo

chu-weer Say's phoebe

chu-weet semipalmated plover

chway red-eyed vireo

chwee chwee chwee chwee chwee American pipit

ch-weet ch-weet Hutton's vireo

ch-wut upland sandpiper

cick-ik-ik-ik white-headed woodpecker

clenk bushtit

click click yellow rail

co-co-co-co-cookachea whip-poor-will

coo-coo band-tailed pigeon

coo-coooo burrowing owl

coo-cuk-cuk-cik-coooo rock dove

coododo brown-headed nuthatch

coo-lee coo-lee common loon

cooo-coo Inca dove

cooo cooo cooo cooo coo coo greater roadrunner

coo-oo sharp-tailed grouse

cree cree cree bald eagle

cronk brant

cruk common raven

cu-cu-cu-cu black-billed cuckoo

cuk cuk cuk great egret

cuk-cuk-cuk-cuk-cuk-cukacheea buff-collared nightjar

cut-cut-turrrrrrrrrrrrr-r marsh wren

dee boreal chickadee

dee-dee-deeerr killdeer

dee deer Siberian tit

deer deer deer deer rufous-crowned sparrow

didididididi snow bunting, least sandpiper

didip Carolina wren

dirrd house wren

dit black-throated blue warbler, dark-eyed junco

drrrt Kentucky warbler

dzay-dzeee Mexican chickadee

dzee-dzee-dzee eastern kingbird

dzeep eastern kingbird

dzeer dzeer dzeer tzee tzee Townsend's warbler

dzeet American dipper, eastern bluebird, eastern meadowlark

dzik common yellowthroat

dzik-dzik American dipper

dzzzt cerulean warbler, worm-eating warbler

ee ee ee ee ee northern beardless-tyrannulet

eeeen eeeen eeeen red-breasted nuthatch

eeeya northern harrier

eek Townsend's solitaire

eenk hooded oriole

ekekekekek harlequin duck

ey-yay ee-yay yellow-throated vireo

fee-be eastern phoebe

fee-bee-ee black-capped chickadee

fee-bee fee-bay Carolina chickadee

fee-bee fee-bee mountain chickadee

few mountain bluebird

few few fawee western bluebird

fi-bee fi-bee black phoebe

fitz-bee alder flycatcher

fitz-bew willow flycatcher

fraaank great blue heron

frrip frrip frrip northern rough-winged swallow

fuss Altamira oriole

gaaaal California gull

ga-ga-ga-ga red-necked grebe

gak gak ga ga ga northern shoveler

garf garf lesser scaup

gar-oo-oo sandhill crane

gaw gaw gaw mangrove cuckoo

ge gadum gaum pied-billed grebe

gek common loon

gerrr Bonaparte's gull

gido ruby-crowned kinglet

git warbling vireo

g-leek California thrasher

glug-glug-glee brown-headed cowbird

go-back go-back go-backa go-back willow ptarmigan

goeet Smith's longspur

gogogogogo king eider

grrrr fish crow

grrrt grrrt canvasback

grrt great kiskadee

gwa gwa gwa harlequin duck

gwit gwit sandwich tern

haa-haa-haa-haa laughing gull

ha-ha-ha-ha-ha yellow-billed loon

ha-ha-ha ha-ha-ha willet

hahahahahaha common loon

haink American bittern

heeh Townsend's solitaire

heenk snow goose

heh heh heh yellow-throated vireo

henk barnacle goose

hew-chew-chew-tsee cerulean warbler

hik eared grebe, MacGillivray's warbler

hiyak hiyar ring-billed gull

honk-a-lonk Canada goose

hoo northern pygmy-owl

hoo hoo hoo hoodoo hoo hoo great horned owl

hoo hoo hoo-hoo, ho hoo hoo-hoo barred owl

hoo hoo hoo hoo hoo boreal owl

hoo-hoohoohoohoo red-billed pigeon

hooip, hooip, hooip common ground-dove

hooo long-eared owl, snowy owl

hoop-a hooo hooo hooo mourning dove

hoot-a-hoot great horned owl

ho-say ma-re-ah greater pewee

houck-houck snow goose

howee western tanager

hoy phainopepla

hulee northern oriole

hup-hup-a-hwooo red-billed pigeon

ik black-headed grosbeak

illy-illy-illy-illy northern hawk-owl

jaaa loggerhead shrike, spot-breasted oriole

jaaay gray jay

jaaeg northern shrike

ja-cob ja-cob acorn woodpecker

jay jay jay blue jay

je-dit je-dit ruby-crowned kinglet

jeee wood duck

jeeeek black-billed magpie

jeet American pipit, arctic warbler, western sandpiper, white-rumped sandpiper

jeew jeew jeew rosy finch

jejejejejeje white-throated swift

jif jif jif jif jif ruddy duck

ji ji ji ji ji mountain plover

jimp sage sparrow, song sparrow

jip Wilson's warbler

jrrr jrrr jrrr white-winged crossbill

jug Scott's oriole

jujujeeeejujeeeju Lincoln's sparrow

juwee hoary redpoll

kaaaaah whooping crane

ka-a-a-ah common black-hawk

kaaa kaaa Barrow's goldeneye

kaah ferruginous hawk

kah red-shouldered hawk

kah-lah-aluck greater white-fronted goose

ka ka ka ka ka hooded merganser

kakakowlp-kowlp yellow-billed cuckoo

kak-kak-kak bald eagle

kak kak kak kak kak long-tailed duck

ka-leep scissor-tailed flycatcher

ka-ronk Canada goose

karrr great egret, red-breasted merganser

karrr karrr greater scaup

karr-r-r common merganser

kar-wit kar-wit gray partridge

kaup kaup kaup black skimmer

ka-whee-oo fulvous whistling duck

kay-ee willet

kay-week kay-week gull-billed tern

kddddrrddi summer tanager

ke white-tailed hawk

ke-deek least tern

kedekekek gray catbird

kee-ah gray partridge, red-shouldered hawk

kee-ar-r-r-r common tern

keeeeeeeeeer red-tailed hawk

keeeel ring-billed gull

keeeer rough-legged hawk

keek long-billed dowitcher, sora

kee-kee-der black rail

keekeekaar bar-tailed godwit

keep-bak scarlet tanager

keer cliff swallow

kee-rer royal tern

kee-rick elegant tern

keer keer arctic tern, marbled murrelet

keewa laughing gull

kee-yow short-eared owl

kee-yur kee-yur kee-yur red-shouldered hawk

kee-zee-ick kee-zee-ick sulphur-bellied flycatcher

kek red-winged blackbird, scissor-tailed flycatcher, yellow-headed blackbird

kekekekeke northern harrier

kek-kek golden-fronted woodpecker

kek kek kek black-necked stilt, common grackle

kek-kek-kek-kek-kek-kek clapper rail, king rail

kemp tricolored blackbird

kep alder flycatcher, sulphur-bellied flycatcher

ker-loo ker-lee-loo whooping crane

kerp kerp ring-necked duck

kerra horned grebe

kerrrr common grackle

ker-seek black tern

ker-wee sora

kewk ruddy turnstone

kiddle chestnut-collared longspur

ki-dee pygmy nuthatch

ki-dit ki-dit brown-headed nuthatch

kid kid kidick kidick Virginia rail

kiilk yellow-bellied flycatcher

kik black tern

ki-ki-dear ki-ki-dear Cassin's kingbird

ki-ki-ki-ki northern hawk-owl

kikikiki great-tailed grackle

kikikikiki downy woodpecker, merlin, whimbrel

ki ki ki kir kir kir white-throated swift

kik kik kik sharp-shinned hawk

kik-kik-kik common gallinule, common tern

kik-kik-kik-kik-kik pileated woodpecker

kil-la white-tailed hawk

killy killy killy American kestrel

kilt canyon towhee

kip pygmy nuthatch, sanderling

kip-ip-ip-ip-ip upland sandpiper crane

kip kip kip common moorhen, wood duck

kip-kip-kip red crossbill, willet

kip kip kip keeaa keeaa red crossbill

kirri-kirri common tern

kis-ka-dee great kiskadee

kit Forster's tern, red-necked phalarope

kit-kit kit pygmy nuthatch

kit-kit-kitter-kitter eastern kingbird

kittick common gallinule

kitti-kitti-kitti least tern

kittip McCown's longspur

kiw kiw kiw sharp-shinned hawk

kkkkkkkk bronzed cowbird, brown-headed cowbird

k-k-k-k-k-k-k-k ruddy turnstone

klaaw herring gull

kleek-kik-ik-ik-ik bald eagle

klee-klee-klee greater yellowlegs

kleep American avocet

kleep kleep American oystercatcher, black oystercatcher

kleerr evening grosbeak

klee-yer northern flicker

kli kli kli kli kli American kestrel

kok least bittern

kok-kok ring-necked pheasant

kokokokok common eider, common merganser

ko-loi-kee northern bobwhite

konk-la-ree red-winged blackbird

kowk Caspian tern

kra-a-a Clark's nutcracker

kraaa black scoter, Caspian tern

kraaaaaah common raven, limpkin

kree dunlin, marbled murrelet

kree-a ferruginous hawk

kreeaaaaaaaaaaaar Swainson's hawk

kree-ah kree-ah kree-ah northern goshawk

kreed green-winged teal

kreed-kreet western grebe

kreee least sandpiper

kreeed Clark's grebe

kree-eep least sandpiper

kreeep Baird's sandpiper

krick-krick western grebe

krik pectoral sandpiper

krr krr krr black rail

krr-onk krr-onk brant

krr-oww limpkin

krrp American coot

krrr mountain plover, plain chachalaca

krrraaak krrraaak surf scoter

krrr kr krrr kr kr anhinga

krrr krrr krrr krrr krrr cactus wren

krrrrrr red-headed woodpecker

kr-r-ruk common moorhen

krrt sedge wren

krut snowy plover

ksh-alee ksh-laa rusty blackbird

ksh-eeee Brewer's blackbird

kuck kuck kuck green heron

kudiloo black-bellied plover

kuk-kuk-cow-cow-cow-cowp-cowp pied-billed grebe

kuk kuk kuk northern goshawk

kuk-kuk-kuk-kuk American coot

ku-ku-ku-ku-ku-ku yellow-billed cuckoo

kurrr California quail

ku-wheet snowy plover

kvik kvik barn swallow

kwa-wee Pacific loon

kwawk black-crowned night-heron

kweek hairy woodpecker, tree swallow

kwesh Florida scrub-jay

kwesh kwesh kwesh Steller's jay

kwok Heermann's gull

kwow Pacific loon

kwow kwow willow ptarmigan

kwuk common loon

kwuk kwuk kwuk red-throated loon

kya golden eagle

kyarr Forster's tern

kyew kyew kyew kyew kyew osprey

kyip kyip kyip black-necked stilt

kyowk green-backed heron

looo-ee poo-too-ee American golden plover

maaaaanh gray catbird

mag mag mag mag mag black-billed magpie

meerr white-eyed vireo

meew black-whiskered vireo, green-tailed towhee

meppp gadwall

mew black-tailed gnatcatcher, gray catbird, pinyon jay, red-eyed vireo

oh-oooo-ooo common eider

oink Virginia rail

o-lo-lee Pacific loon

on-kee-kaahn tricolored blackbird

ooaah coo coo coo mourning dove

oo-ah barred owl

ooah ooah pectoral sandpiper

oo-eeek oo-eeek wood duck

oo-eek eared grebe

oo-loo-woo greater prairie-chicken

oonk-a-lunk American bittern

owiiil-ka owiiil-ka owiiil-ka arctic loon

ow-oo-ur common eider

ow-owdle-ow long-tailed duck

pa-chip-chip-chip American goldfinch

paint peent peent peent American woodcock

pa-teek Nuttall's woodpecker

pay hermit thrush

pdzeeeee rock wren

pee vermilion flycatcher

pee-a-weee eastern wood-pewee

pee-dew pee-dew pee-dew buff-breasted flycatcher

pee-ee Say's phoebe

peeeer western wood-pewee

pee-eet common nighthawk

peeeew black scoter

peee-yuk northern beardless-tyrannulet

pee-ik common goldeneye, common nighthawk

peek hairy woodpecker, Hammond's flycatcher, rose-breasted
  grosbeak

peek peek peek Abert's towhee

pee-krrr-krrr hairy woodpecker

peenk brown towhee

peent American woodcock, common nighthawk

peep alder flycatcher, blue-winged teal

peep-lo piping plover

peep peep gull-billed tern

peer northern beardless-tyrannulet

peet Acadian flycatcher, solitary sandpiper, white-winged
  crossbill

peeta peeta peeta Mexican chickadee

pee-teee broad-winged hawk

peet-seet, peet-suh, peet Acadian flycatcher

peet-weet spotted sandpiper

peet-weet-weet solitary sandpiper

peeur dusky-capped flycatcher

pee-wee pee-peoo black phoebe

pee-widdi eastern wood-pewee

peew peew peew peew peew tufted titmouse

pee-yer western wood-pewee

pek pek pek Cooper's hawk

pep pep pep peer peer peer common moorhen

per-chik-o-ree American goldfinch

per-wee yellow-bellied flycatcher

peter peter peter olive warbler

pe-tip pe-tip Swainson's hawk

pew eastern bluebird, Lapland longspur, western bluebird

pe-wee-ah snowy plover

pew pew purple martin

phew veery

pichew pichew chew chew chew northern cardinal

pidididid pine grosbeak

pik black-backed woodpecker, black-headed grosbeak, downy
woodpecker, ladder-backed woodpecker, lazuli bunting, purple
finch, red phalarope, three-toed woodpecker

pill-will-willet willet

pil-pil greater pewee

pink McCown's longspur, white-crowned sparrow

pip olive-sided flycatcher

pip-pip water pipit

pip pip pip olive-sided flycatcher

pip-pip-pip greater pewee, piping plover

pip-pip-pip-pip tropical kingbird

pit Botteri's sparrow, olive warbler

pit-a-see pit-a-see vermilion flycatcher

pitchoorip crissal thrasher

pit-er-ik western tanager

pit pit pit wood thrush

pitpitpitpitpit curve-billed thrasher

pit-pit-pit-tr-r-r-r wrentit

pit-sit horned lark

pi-tup-zeee grasshopper sparrow

pi-weer pi-wee Say's phoebe

pleeek black-necked stilt

plick sanderling

plid-plid northern shrike

plik Canada warbler

plik-plik-plik sanderling

plit eastern wood-pewee

pluk western meadowlark

poopoopoo least bittern

poo-pup Inca dove

poor-will common poorwill

poor-will-ip common poorwill

po po po black-billed cuckoo

popopopopo wood thrush

po po po po po po po po boreal owl

pree-pree-prrreeit dusky-capped flycatcher

prek prek red-breasted merganser
prit-wheer ash-throated flycatcher
prreeet great crested flycatcher
prrip prrip northern pintail
prrk prrk bufflehead
prrrrk American crow
prrrt ash-throated flycatcher, Nuttall's woodpecker
prrruk common raven
pseet-trip-pseet western flycatcher
psssss red-throated pipit
pulip pulip upland sandpiper
pup pup pup pup pup scissor-tailed flycatcher
pur pur wheeer common pauraque
purreeer brown-crested flycatcher
purr-eet thick-billed kingbird
puwi scarlet tanager
pwee blue-gray gnatcatcher
pweech painted bunting
pweeeeee broad-winged hawk
pweee pweee red-tailed hawk
pweest Acadian flycatcher
pwich mourning warbler
pwid pwid pwid too too too kre lark bunting
pwik Connecticut warbler
pwip pwip pwip ferruginous pygmy-owl
pwit buff-breasted flycatcher
pzrrrt Hammond's flycatcher

qua-ack American wigeon

quack American black duck, blue-winged teal, bufflehead, canvasback, common goldeneye, gadwall, mallard, northern pintail, northern shoveler, white-winged scoter

quack quack quack American black duck, bufflehead, mallard

quark yellow-crowned night-heron

quee-ah Swainson's thrush

quee-ark mountain quail

queedle American golden plover

queedle queedle loggerhead shrike

queedle-queedle-queedle blue jay

queeep queeep quee quee quee American oystercatcher

quee-lick smoth-billed ani

queer tropical kingbird

queh queh queh pinyon jay

querp stilt sandpiper

quick-quick-quick burrowing owl

quitta quitto quitta quitto great crested flycatcher

quok black-crowned night-heron

raaaaaah Caspian tern

raaaa raaaa little blue heron

raaang ruddy duck

raarr snowy egret

rad rad rad rad yellow-headed blackbird

ree-dee-dee-dee-dee Hutton's vireo

reek-a-der plain chachalaca

rehk rehk rehk peregrine falcon

rik snowy owl

scaip common snipe

scaup lesser scaup

scraa scraa scraa northern jacana

screeeeeeee barn owl

see-dee-dee-dee Carolina chickadee

seedle seedle seedle chup chup hermit warbler

seee brown creeper

seeeee seeee seeee Harris's sparrow

seeeep Brewer's sparrow, red-throated pipit

seeeew cedar waxwing

seee slip slip slip Bachman's sparrow

seek blue-throated hummingbird, ovenbird

see-lip verdin

seeoo rose-throated becard

seep-seep black-and-white warbler

seep seep seep blue-throated hummingbird

see-ree calliope hummingbird

see-see-see-tip-eecha chestnut-sided warbler

see see see titi see brown creeper

see-seet-seet-seet-seet trrrrr yellow-rumped warbler

seet orange-crowned warbler, pine warbler, yellow-throated
warbler

seet-say Blackburnian warbler

seet seet seet seet Cape May warbler

see-weet Nashville warbler

shaack shaack shaack Steller's jay

shack-shack loggerhead shrike, northern shrike

shing-a-ring-a-ring-a Sprague's pipit

shreeep Florida scrub-jay

shrrrr marsh wren

sillit tsurrp sillit seet dusky flycatcher

sip-a-tik Henslow's sparrow

si-si-seeeeee-soo-see Cassin's sparrow

skeeeh northern mockingbird

skeew green heron

skee we we blue-winged teal, cinnamon teal

skelp skelp skelp green heron

skwak redhead

slip American pipit

smack dark-eyed junco, fox sparrow

snik blue-winged warbler

spik bushtit, indigo bunting, Louisiana waterthrush, pyrrhuloxia, Strickland's woodpecker, varied bunting

spwik northern waterthrush

squeer squeer red-headed woodpecker

squeet Sprague's pipit

sreee Bohemian waxwing, cedar waxwing

sripp red-cockaded woodpecker

ssit yellow-rumped warbler

ssllick Henslow's sparrow

stik Tennessee warbler

stip black-chinned sparrow, black-throated blue warbler, dark-eyed junco, Savannah sparrow, yellow-eyed junco

stit Anna's hummingbird

sweeep red phalarope

swee-swee-swee-weeterrrr black-chinned sparrow

sweet sweet vesper sparrow, lazuli bunting

sweet-sweet chew-chew indigo bunting

sweet sweet sweet song sparrow

swit black-throated green warbler, clay-colored sparrow, hermit warbler

szee barn swallow

tak violet-crowned hummingbird

tau red-throated pipit

tchew black-chinned hummingbird

tchik white wagtail

teedle-oo American tree sparrow

teeev harlequin duck

tee-ew tew tew tew tew yellow-throated warbler

tee-ho groove-billed ani

teek Abert's towhee

teep Baird's sparrow, Cassin's sparrow, fox sparrow, hooded warbler, Swainson's warbler

tee-seet cordilleran flycatcher

tees teesi teesi bay-breasted warbler

teeteetee black-throated sparrow

tee tee tee tew tew canyon wren

tee too tee tee verdin

teeu Altamira oriole

tee-wee tee-wee tee-wee t-shee canyon wren

teew teew tew tew tewtew titit field sparrow

tee-yar eastern meadowlark

tee-yer tee-yer lesser goldfinch

tek black-throated green warbler, golden-crowned warbler, northern wheatear

terp five-striped sparrow

tetek broad-billed hummingbird

tew lesser yellowlegs, snow bunting

tewp olive warbler

tew-tew-tew greater yellowlegs, pine grosbeak

tew-tew-tew-tew-tew-tee-tee Grace's warbler

thew evening grosbeak

ti Cape May warbler

tick-ear rock wren

tickety-tshshshsh-tick Le Conte's sparrow

ticki-tick-tew Lapland longspur

tick-tick winter wren

tick tick tick grasshopper sparrow

tic-tic-tic-tic-tic clapper rail

tic-tic tic-tic-tic tic-tic yellow rail

tidik black-capped vireo

tidio Cassin's finch

tik cordilleran flycatcher, northern cardinal, song sparrow

tik-tikikikikikit pyrrhuloxia

tilk Wilson's warbler

ting ting ting bluethroat

tink blue grosbeak, Costa's hummingbird, lark sparrow

tink-oo Lawrence's goldfinch

tip black-throated gray warbler, black-throated sparrow, golden-crowned kinglet

tip-tip-tip rufous-winged sparrow

tip-tip-tiptip-tip sage sparrow

tirri tirri torri torri mourning warbler

tirup Bendire's thrasher

tit-i-tit pine siskin

ti ti ti ti ti Acadian flycatcher

t-k-k-k-k-k-k white-rumped sandpiper

tleee teee-eee lesser goldfinch

tlee-oo-ee black-bellied plover

toit-toit-toit crissal thrasher

tok common raven

too-ee too-ee too-ee semipalmated plover

too-err Lawrence's goldfinch

took ferruginous pygmy-owl, northern bobwhite, varied thrush

toop-toop-toop-toop-toop yellow-breasted chat

tootoo white-breasted nuthatch

too too too too too too northern saw-whet owl

too-too-too-too-too-took-took northern pygmy-owl

to to to to to whimbrel

toto-zeee toto-zeee calliope hummingbird

tourreee royal tern

tri-i-i-p cordilleran flycatcher

trit-weet trit-weet trit-weet tree swallow

trrit northern rough-winged swallow

trrrrk wrentit

tr-tee-ar arctic tern

tschizzick white wagtail

tse-beek Hammond's flycatcher

tsee Baird's sparrow, black phoebe

tsee-ee horned lark

tseeeer European starling

tseeew field sparrow

tseek-a-dee-dee chestnut-backed chickadee

tseek-day-day boreal chickadee

tseep western flycatcher, white-crowned sparrow

tseer violet-green swallow

tseet Lucy's warbler, Tennessee warbler, white-throated sparrow

tsee-titi horned lark

tsee tsee tsee golden-crowned kinglet

tsee tsee tsee tew tew ruby-crowned kinglet

tsee-tsee-tsee-tsee-tsirr American redstart

tsew American tree sparrow

tsick Blackburnian warbler, red-cockaded woodpecker

tsick-a-der-der plain titmouse

tsiip chipping sparrow, hooded warbler

tsink palm warbler

tsip Bachman's sparrow, Brewer's sparrow, lark sparrow

tsip-tsip-tsipsi yellow wagtail

tsip tsip tsip titi tisi Blackburnian warbler

tss prairie warbler

tsssuk brown thrasher

ts ts ts ts ts violet-crowned hummingbird

tsuk marsh wren

tsweeet American redstart

tsweep yellow wagtail

tswee-tee-teet western wood-pewee

tsyoo-tsyoo-tsyoo yellow-throated warbler

t-t-t-t-t-t-t-t rock dove, ruby-throated hummingbird

tt tt tt tt lark bunting

t-t-t-t-t-t-t-t-klaaaaar limpkin

ttttttttt killdeer

t-t-t-tzeee-tzz Savannah sparrow

tuk red-faced warbler, yellow-breasted chat

tuptup-sheeeeee saltmarsh sharp-tailed sparrow

tut tut tut American robin

tu-tu-tu short-billed dowitcher

tu-tu-tu tu-tu-tu-tu elf owl

twee warbling vireo

twee do-do-do-do semipalmated sandpiper

twee-ee-ee Aleutian tern

tweeep Le Conte's thrasher

twee-twee-teeeo hooded warbler

twee twee twee spotted sandpiper

twit-twit-twit northern waterthrush

twi twi twi downy woodpecker

twitwitwititit merlin

tyik-tyik white-winged crossbill

tyoo-tyoo lesser yellowlegs

tyuk rufous hummingbird, rusty blackbird

tzee tree swallow

tzeedl-tzeedl-tzeedl-tee-tee-tee cerulean warbler

tzeen tzeen tzeen yellow wagtail

tzeet dark-eyed junco

tzee tzee-a Sprague's pipit

tzee tzee tzee bushtit

tzew-zuppity-zuppity-zup rufous hummingbird

tzip Baird's sparrow

tzzz bay-breasted warbler, blackpoll warbler

urrrrah northern gannet

veer veery

veer veer veer veer veery

vidervidi vidervidi warbling vireo

vidididididi western meadowlark

vit barn swallow

vvvvit painted bunting

vvvvvvvvvvvvvvvv least grebe

waaaw California quail

waaow redhead

wack-wack-wack least bittern

wah-up common ground-dove

wah wah wah wah greater white-fronted goose

wak-wak-wak Virginia rail

waow short-eared owl

warr warr warr American wigeon

way-urrr horned grebe

we-chew Smith's longspur

we-chew we-chew we-chew peregrine falcon

wee-ah gray-cheeked thrush

wee-bee alder flycatcher

weedle-eedle blue jay

weee great kiskadee

weee-a Gambel's quail, sora

weee weee weee weee Philadelphia vireo

weeip Le Conte's thrasher

week gray-breasted jay

weeoo black-headed grosbeak

wee-see black-and-white warbler

weet hepatic tanager, willow flycatcher

weeta weeta weeta che che che Lucy's warbler

weeta weeta weeta wee painted redstart

weet weet weet spotted sandpiper

weet-weet-weet-weet-zee-zee yellow warbler

weety-weety-weeteo magnolia warbler

weety weety weety plain titmouse

weeweeweewee Clark's grebe

wee-zee wee-zee wee-zee wee-zee black-and-white warbler

weezy weezy weezy zee Townsend's warbler

wenk wenk wenk wenk black-billed magpie

what-cheer what-cheer pyrrhuloxia

wheeer orchard oriole

wheeoo gray jay

wheep great crested flycatcher

wheep wheep wheep black oystercatcher

wheerr house finch

whee-seet western flycatcher

wheet American avocet, bluethroat

whee-wheeoo-titi-whee gray-cheeked thrush

whee whee whee Swainson's warbler

whew-whew-whew lesser yellowlegs

whididid Aleutian tern

whidoo Steller's jay

whip-poor-will whip-poor-will

whip wee deeer olive-sided flycatcher

whit brown-crested flycatcher, dusky-capped flycatcher, dusky
flycatcher, gray flycatcher, least flycatcher, Swainson's thrush,
western kingbird, Wilson's plover

whitoo chukar

whit-weet curve-billed thrasher

whit-will-do brown-crested flycatcher

whi-whi-whi-whi-whi white-breasted nuthatch

whoit wi wit yellow-breasted chat

whook mountain quail

whooleeeee wheelooooo upland sandpiper

whoooee European starling

whoo-whoo band-tailed pigeon

whoo whoo whoo   great gray owl

whu   stilt sandpiper

whup whup whup   spotted owl

wichity-wichity-wichity-witch   common yellowthroat

wicka wicka wicka   black-tailed godwit, common snipe

widdik pik widdik pik pik pik   western kingbird

wik-wik-wik-wik   northern flicker

wink   Harris's sparrow

wit wit weee drr drr drr   bank swallow

wit-wit-wee wit-wit-wee   American golden plover

wi-wi-whew   American wigeon

woc   black-crowned night-heron, yellow-crowned night-heron

woo-ho woo-woo woo-ho   tundra swan

woooip   long-eared owl

woo-oo woo-oo   common ground-dove

wrrrep   hooded merganser

wuck-a-wuck-a-wuck-a   pileated woodpecker

wuk wuk   pileated woodpecker

wulla wulla wulla   snowy egret

wunk   Wilson's phalarope

wurp   phainopepla

yaa yaa yaa   double-crested cormorant

yank   white-breasted nuthatch

yeeb   mallard

yek   Heermann's gull

yep   black skimmer

yink red-breasted nuthatch

yip yip yip Gila woodpecker

yip-yip-yip black-necked stilt

yoww Heermann's gull

yuk-yuk-yuk-yuk-yuckle-yuckle herring gull

zaryp cliff swallow

za-za-za gull-billed tern

zeedl zeedl zeedl golden-cheeked warbler

zeeeee canyon towhee

zeeeeeeeee-up northern parula

zeeer red-winged blackbird

zeeet Lincoln's sparrow, rufous-crowned sparrow, swamp
  sparrow

zeeeweeee eastern towhee, spotted towhee

zeee zeee zeee cedar waxwing

zee-o-eet Abert's towhee

zeeooee seaside sparrow

zeet-zeet-zeet blue-gray gnatcatcher

zee zee zee zee zee prairie warbler

zereesh green-tailed towhee

zheee zheee zheee clay-colored sparrow

zhe-zhe-zhe-zhe-zhe palm warbler

zhreeee black-capped vireo, pine siskin

zhweeee hermit thrush

zhwee zhwee zhwee Carolina wren

zidza zidza zidza black-throated gray warbler

zik arctic warbler

zing broad-billed hummingbird, Costa's hummingbird

zink plumbous vireo

zip northern parula

zi-zi-zi-zi-zeee blackpoll warbler, golden-winged warbler

zoo zee zoo zoo zee black-throated green warbler

zra-ap roseate tern

zreee house finch

zreeeeek least tern

zrink Bewick's wren

zrrt snow bunting

zrr-zrr-zrr-zrr-zrree Brewer's sparrow

zrurrr Forster's tern

zttttttttt eastern meadowlark

zur zur zur zree black-throated blue warbler

zweet zweet zweet prothonotary warbler

zzip northern waterthrush

zzzzzd lazuli bunting

15. Birds may rehearse phrases they later discard from their repertoire.

16. Occasionally a bird will introduce some freak sound and make it part of its song.

Lexicon for Great Britain and Northern Europe

aaa jay

a-aadelow long-tailed duck

aaak roseate tern

aaarr razorbill

a-ahulee long-tailed duck

aahung-ung-ung greylag goose

aark-aark shelduck

aar-orr-kakarr ptarmigan

aarr puffin

aarrk bittern

ach ach roseate tern

ag-ag-ag shelduck

ag ag ag ag arrr fulmar

ah-hee-oo eider

ahng whooper swan

ah-oo eider

ah-ooo-oo great northern diver

ak-ak-ak-ak shelduck

ang-ang-ank pink-footed goose

aouk great black-backed gull

ark barnacle goose

arp-arp corncrake

arra guillemot

arrah gannet

arr-ou-er puffin

arrr ptarmigan

bibibibee little grebe

boobooboo short-eared owl

but but bullfinch

b'wump bittern

caw rook

cch-huck pochard

chaarr hoopoe

cha-chak golden pheasant

chack-chack fieldfare, red-backed shrike, wheatear

chack chack chack crossbill, magpie, ring ouzel

chack-chee-uk red-backed shrike

chak golden pheasant, jackdaw

charr lesser whitethroat, whitethroat

charr-charr-charr great skua

chat stonechat

check garden warbler

chee Cetti's warbler, kingfisher

chee-aw chough

chee-chee-chee redpoll

chee cheweecho-weecho-weecho-wee Cetti's warbler

cheechiwee-cheechiweechoo-chiwichoo whitethroat

chee-ip house sparrow

chee-kee kingfisher

cheep osprey

chee-ree-ree swift

chew Lapland bunting

chew-it spotted redshank

chewk osprey

chichichichit greenfinch, linnet

chick brambling, Cetti's warbler, great spotted woodpecker, lesser spotted woodpecker, little stint, tree sparrow

chick-chick-chick-chick blackbird

chiff yellowhammer

chiff-chaff chiffchaff

chiff-if wood sandpiper

chika-ke-ke-ke marsh tit

chik-ka-chik-ka snipe

chikka-chikka-chikka-chikka-chikk lesser whitethroat

chink reed bunting

chip chaffinch, corn bunting, greenshank

chip-chip crossbill

chip chip chip tree sparrow

chip-chip-chip-chip-chip-chip-chip marsh tit

chip-chip-chip-chwee-chwee-tissi-chooeeo chaffinch

chipper-chipper-chipper snipe

chippoo-it tio-tew tutee-o wee-ploo-ploo tu-itty song thrush

chirr Dartford warbler

chirr chirr chirr-r-r crested tit

chirrick chiffchaff

chirr-ik-tik Dartford warbler

chirrip curlew sandpiper

chirrp house martin

chirrup skylark

chit chit Dartford warbler

chit-chit-chit little stint

chittuck redwing

chit-up yellow wagtail

chivee tawny pipit

chook nightingale

chook chook magpie

choor-r-r crested tit

chreek house sparrow

chrr nightingale

chrr-chrr chiffchaff

cht cht bearded tit

chuc-chuc-chuc brambling

chuchuchu greenfinch

chuch-uch-uch redpoll

chuck chuck black grouse

chuff chough

chuik roseate tern

chuka-chuka red-legged partridge

chuk-uk ruff

chuk-uk-uk   hen harrier

chup   redwing

churr   blackcap, icterine warbler, pochard, reed warbler, scoter, sedge warbler

chur-r-r   wren

chuup   greenfinch

chwee   yellowhammer

chweek   twite

chwit-chwit   nuthatch

clink   dipper

cluck   raven

cock   coot

cock-cock   capercaillie

colk-chack-chack   red-legged partridge

coo-cooo-cuk   collared dove

coo-cooooo-coo   collared dove

coo-coo-roo-c-coo   wood pigeon

coo-ic   nightjar

coo-oo-er   stock dove

coo-ree   stone curlew

coor-loo   scoter

coo-roo   stock dove

coo-roo-uh   eider

coour-lee   curlew

cree-a cree-a   little ringed plover

crek-crek   corncrake

cuc-coo cuckoo

currah tufted duck

curruc moorhen

deedeedleleddwee-daaa siskin

deederoid icterine warbler

deedl-eedl-eedl wood sandpiper

deep-deep-deep bluethroat

didlihn tawny pipit

dirrdirrdrrrt little stint

djadjadja twite

due bullfinch

dzee-dzee-dzee-dzee willow tit

dzer whitethroat

dzwee brambling

eest-eest meadow pipit

ee woomp bittern

ek-ek teal

ergh-ergh snowy owl

er-oook-ka-ka-ka-ka ptarmigan

erz-erz-erz willow tit

frarnk grey heron

ga red-necked grebe

gack-gack arctic skua

gag Iceland gull

gag-gag-gag lesser black-backed gull

gak-gak-gak glaucous gull

gak-owk-ow-kyow-yowk great black-backed gull

gep-gep water rail

gobak-gobak-gobak-bak-bak red grouse

gog Iceland gull

gok-gok-gok-gok eider

gorr great crested grebe

greck great crested grebe

grraa-grraa sand martin

grrr hronk brent goose

grutto black-tailed godwit

gugnunc pink-footed goose

gung great crested grebe

gwoo-err guillemot

hah-hah-hah great skua

heea-hi-hi-hi-heea red kite

heeee-yoch-hyoch-och glaucous gull

hicker-whicker black-necked grebe

hihihi pochard

hirruc-chirruc-chirruc-teer-tuk-tuk-tuk-jag-churr-churr reed
  warbler

hoia tufted duck

honk carrion crow

hoo Bewick's swan

hoo-eet willow warbler

hooeet redstart

hooh-hoo-hoo-hoo stock dove

hoo-hoo-oo-hoooooo tawny owl

hoop-ah whooper swan

hoop-poo-poo hoopoe

hoorh snowy owl

houeet Bonelli's warbler

howk Bewick's swan

huhuhuhuhuhuhu snipe

hukhukkukkuk Bewick's swan

hwee red-breasted flycatcher

hweet bluethroat, chiffchaff, nightingale

hweet-tuc-tuc redstart

hwet hwet hwet spotted crake

if-he if-he if-he coal tit

jack garganey, jackdaw

jag-jag-jag-kerr-kerr-kerr reed warbler

jee crossbill

jik jik great crested grebe

jip jip crossbill

kaa chough

kaaa jay

kaah rook

kack kack gadwall

kajak bean goose

kak-ak-ak great skua

ka ka ka ka magpie

kak-kak-kak peregrine

karr karr scaup

karrk-karrk pheasant

kar-r-r red-breasted merganser

karrr goosander, reed warbler

kar-wic grey partridge

kau kau bittern

ke-ak barn owl

keck keck red-necked grebe

kee-aa lesser black-backed gull

keearrr common tern

kee-aw short-eared owl

keeaw jackdaw

kee-errk peregrine

kee-kee arctic tern

kee kee kee kestrel, merlin

kee-kee-kee-kee lesser spotted woodpecker

kee-oo marsh harrier

kee-orrh korrh-korrh-korrh Iceland gull

kee-ow glaucous gull, Mediterranean gull

keeow common gull

keerk carrion crow

kee-wick tawny owl

kee-yah arctic tern, common gull, common tern

kek great crested grebe, kestrel, linnet

kekekeke Montagu's harrier

ke-ke-ke-ke-ke hen harrier

kek-kek black-headed gull

kekkekkek sparrowhawk

kek-kek-kek-kek peregrine

ker-honk Canada goose

kerr kerr goosander

kew-kew-kew hobby

kewkewkewkewkew green woodpecker

khreei barn owl

ki-aow arctic skua

kiaow kiaow lesser black-backed gull

kicowk coot

kiew kiew little owl

kik common tern, merlin, middle spotted woodpecker

kik-ik-ik merlin

kikikikikik-kik-kik-kik moorhen

kik kek gep krui tik pit kviu kve tchif tchuf water rail

kik-kik black tern

kik kik kik kestrel

kik-kik-kik hobby

kik-kik-kirra arctic tern

ki-och-ki-och-ki-och herring gull

ki-och-yoch-yoch-yoch lesser black-backed gull

kip-kip-kip oystercatcher

kipp kipp kipp water rail

kirik hobby

kirr black tern

kirrick Sandwich tern

kirri kirri common tern

kirri kirri kirri little tern

kirrr-ik kirrr-ik grey partridge

kitititit turnstone

kit-kit little tern

kit-kit-keerr common tern

kittac moorhen

kitt-ee-wake kittiwake

kiwick woodchat shrike

kja golden eagle

kjikjikji peregrine

kleep avocet

kleep-kleep oystercatcher

klee weet green sandpiper

klerreb garganey

klooit avocet

klu-ludle-lu-ludle-lu-ludle green sandpiper

knack garganey

knot knot

kokkok black-throated diver

kok-ok capercaillie

kok ok ok ok red grouse

kor-r shelduck

korr cormorant

korrk-kok pheasant

korronk raven

ko wee ou magpie

kowk coot

kow-kow white-fronted goose

kraak golden oriole

kraa kraa kraa carrion crow

krair nutcracker

krarnk grey heron

kree-ah black-headed gull

kree-ik little tern

krek gadwall

krikrikri grey partridge

kritt teal

krokrokro pintail

kronk grey heron

krooihf water rail

krreet pectoral sandpiper

krrook brent goose

kr-r-r eider

kr-r-rk moorhen

krrrr red-breasted merganser

krru-wit-tew black-tailed godwit

krrx-krrx corncrake

kuk black-headed gull

kuk-ku-hoo-coo Manx shearwater

kuk-kuk red-legged partridge

kuk kwuk red-throated diver

kuk-uk-uk ptarmigan, ruff

kurr kurr goldeneye

kur-r-r pochard, scoter, tufted duck

kurrr nightingale

kut kut kuttuc pheasant

kviell lesser grey shrike

kvi-kvi-kvi curlew

kwa-kwa-kwa ptarmigan

kwar kwar woodcock

kwarr black-headed gull

kwarrp carrion crow

kwee hobby

kweeoo marsh harrier

kweep merlin

kwic-we-wic quail

kwih marsh harrier

kwitaleeyu ringed plover

kwit-it corn bunting, knot

kwoi-kwoi dunlin

kwowk short-eared owl

kwuk kwuk kwuk black-throated diver, great northern diver, red-throated diver

kwuk-uk-uk chough

kwup black-headed gull

kya jackdaw

kyee-kyee-owkyowkyowk lesser black-backed gull

kyeu-kyeu-kyeu wryneck

kyew chough

kyow kyow herring gull
kyow-kyow-gah-gah-gah herring gull

lok-toggi lok-toggi jack snipe
loudl-oudl-ow long-tailed duck
lu-lu-lu-lu-lu woodlark
lyo-lyok white-fronted goose

meeoo peeoo buzzard
mink-mink-mink blackbird

nheck gadwall

og barnacle goose
ook little owl
oo-oo little owl
oo-oo-oo long-eared owl
oo-roo-coo rock dove
oo-roo-oo stock dove
oor-oor-roo-coo rock dove
orrrt-orrrt woodcock
ow-ow-ow long-tailed duck

parr-harr-harr puffin
pee-a honey buzzard
peeeeee black guillemot
peek-kapeek oystercatcher
pee-oo jay, nightingale
pee-pee-pee arctic tern

pee-pee-pee-pee lesser spotted woodpecker

pee-pirri-pee ring ouzel

peep-peep dotterel

peep peep peep meadow pipit

peep-peep-peep-peep rock pipit

peerrweet-weet-weet lapwing

pee-u goldfinch, little ringed plover, ring ouzel

peeu snow bunting

pee-u-pee-u-pee-u little ringed plover

pee-wit lapwing

pee-yow buzzard

peu bullfinch

pew sparrowhawk

pew-ee-ew honey buzzard

phwit little grebe

pick-perwick quail

pik raven

ping ping bearded tit

pink chaffinch

pit-a-lee-o pit-a-lee-o ringed plover

pitcheu marsh tit

piu-piu-piu willow tit, wood warbler

plue-plue-plue green woodpecker

poo-eep black-necked grebe

poo-poo-poo hoopoe

preep teal

prreeo arctic tern

pruk raven

psee-ee Montagu's harrier

ptick song thrush

ptsee blackbird

puk-kuk-kuk-oo Manx shearwater

purr-r purr-r purr-r turtle dove

pwee pwee pwee mistle thrush

pzik-ik hawfinch

quack garganey, goldeneye, mallard, shoveler, teal

qua qua qua herring gull

quark mallard, moorhen

queek mallard

queep ringed plover

quee quee quee wryneck

quee-quee-skir dotterel

quee-reek goldeneye

quek ek mallard

quer-r-r gadwall

queu-queu-queu-queu green woodpecker

quic-ic-ic quail

quick quick oystercatcher

quickquickquickquick cuckoo

qu-it roseate tern

quit quit sanderling

quooick nightjar

quuck quuck pintail

raa-ka-ka-ka red grouse

rah-rah-rah great crested grebe

raib mallard

rak rak rak rak wigeon

ree-oo-too-oo ree-oo-too-oo greenshank

reeta black-tailed godwit

rek-kek-kek red grouse

rick-rick-rick snowy owl

rok-rok-rok red-breasted merganser

rookoo black grouse

roor-rrr turtle dove

rott rott brent goose

rronk brent goose

rroorrrrr rroorrrrr rroorrrrr turtle dove

rrrr redpoll

rruk brent goose

scape snipe

seea-seea-seea tree pipit

seeerrrr grasshopper warbler

seeh fieldfare

seeip redwing

seep dunnock

seeto-seeto-seeto coal tit

shee-ik shick ick red-backed shrike

shrreee wood warbler

shushushushu magpie

sip black redstart, tree pipit

sipp song thrush

sip sip dipper

sipsipsipteezeteezeteeze tree pipit

sirrr waxwing

si si si great tit

si-si-si crested tit

sissi-sissi-sip cirl bunting

si-ut-ut-si-re-ut-ut-ut bullfinch

si-wick woodcock

siz-eet grey wagtail

skaap jack snipe

skerr great skua

skraaak jay

sku-arr arctic skua

soo-shoo-oo long-eared owl

spatt starling

srihb tree pipit

ssrih treecreeper

ssu-ik-ik-ik Lady Amherst's pheasant

stip stip stip stip-stip-stip-stip-shreeeee wood warbler

stirrrrrup wren

swee yellow-browed warbler

sweer-sweeree swift

tac tac bluethroat, garden warbler

tac-tac-tac ring ouzel

tak tak nightingale, whitethroat

tak-tak-tak blackcap, tree sparrow

taludl-taludl-taludl golden plover

taweeo taweeo taweeo redshank

tchack barred warbler, blackcap

tchak fieldfare, jackdaw, lesser whitethroat

tcharrr barred warbler

tchay tchay willow tit

tchay-tchay marsh tit

tcheee reed bunting

tcheer starling

tche-wik tche-wi-i-i-i-ck turnstone

tchick grasshopper warbler, great spotted woodpecker

tching-tching bearded tit

tchip-tchip-tchi-cheek osprey

tchirrek red-necked phalarope

tchirrip house martin, sand martin

tchirrp shore lark

tchirr-r Dartford warbler

tchizzick pied wagtail

tchook tchook tchook blackbird

tch-sheew black grouse

tchuitt spotted redshank

tchuk blackbird, ring ouzel, song thrush

tchup tree sparrow

tearr sand martin

teck icterine warbler

tee aw ti too ee mistle thrush

teecha-teecha-teecha great tit

teeeu whimbrel

teek teek tur whee whee hawfinch

teeo roseate tern

tee-oo wood warbler

tee tee tee sissi-tee treecreeper

teeu Lapland bunting, little ringed plover

teez tree pipit

tek tek tree sparrow

terjee crossbill

teu greenfinch, ortolan bunting, redshank, snow bunting

teu-i-teu-i-teu-i greenshank

teuk teuk teuk redshank

teu teu teu teu house sparrow

tewk coot

tew tew tew greenshank

tic melodious warbler, pied flycatcher

tick tack spotted crake

ticky-tik-ticky-tik Lapland bunting

tic-tic robin, whinchat

tic-tic-tic wren

tik Dartford warbler

tik-a-tik-tik arctic skua

tink-tink-tink-eida-eida-eida-hwee-da-hwee-da red-breasted
flycatcher

tiriririp snow bunting

tirra-lira skylark

tirrititt serin

tirr-pee-oo golden plover

tissip meadow pipit

tit little stint

titi-ri dotterel

titirri-titirri-tit common sandpiper

tititic black redstart

titititit turnstone

titsissi-sissi-sissi coal tit

titti-titti-titti whimbrel

titti-turee-turee snow bunting

titti-weeti common sandpiper

tiutiu-tiutiutiuk-swee yellowhammer

t-keep t-keep redshank

tleea-tleea-tleea wood sandpiper

tlee-oo golden plover

tlee-oo-ee grey plover

tlip ortolan bunting

tlooeet-tlooeet-to-tlooeet black-throated diver

tlui golden plover

tlu-leu-leu redshank

tock raven

too-eet willow warbler

tooi ringed plover

tooick redstart

took redwing, wren

took took shoveler

took-took arctic skua

too-li ringed plover

toolooeet toolooeet toolooeet woodlark

toy toy nuthatch

treap dunlin

trree snow bunting

trritrrit house martin

trrr wigeon, wren

trrrr Lapland bunting

tr-weet stonechat

tsak tsak stonechat

tscheeta tscheeta woodlark

tschk ring ouzel

tschreck red-legged partridge

tsee robin, treecreeper

tseek dunnock, reed bunting

tseek-teet-teu-tississisk reed bunting

tseek-tseek-tseek-shnirlrlrl corn bunting

tseep meadow pipit

tsee-seep shore lark

tsee-tsee coal tit

tsee-tsee-ch-ch-ch-ch blue tit

tsee-tsee-tsee-tsit blue tit

tsee-tsreep yellow wagtail

tsee-tui great tit

tsee-wee-wee common sandpiper

tserret-et-et-et blue tit

tse weep yellow wagtail

tsink great tit

tsip ortolan bunting, robin, water pipit

tsip-tsip-tsip-tsip rock pipit

tsirr yellow wagtail

tsirrp long-tailed tit

tsissup shore lark

tsit nuthatch, treecreeper

tsit-siwee **tsi-wichoo** shore lark

tsiwick woodcock

tsoo-ee starling

tsooeet greenfinch, linnet, redpoll

tswee greenfinch

tsweek brambling

tsweet twite

tswik Savi's warbler

tswit-tswit swallow

tswitt-tswitt goldfinch

tsy-zi siskin

tucc-tucc black redstart

tuc-tuc sedge warbler, spotted flycatcher

tuc-tuc-tuc mistle thrush

tukatuk turnstone

tuktuk shoveler

tu-loo-ee green sandpiper

tu-reep pied wagtail

tur-ee-tur black-tailed godwit

turr dunlin

tut long-tailed tit

tu-tic-tic whinchat

tu-whit ruff, tawny owl

tu-yu-yu redshank

twee-o golden eagle

t-weet swallow

twee-tee-too crested lark

twee-twee-twee nuthatch

twee-wee-wee common sandpiper

twick twick sanderling

twink yellowhammer

twip redwing

twiri-diri-tiri-wiri little tern

twirr-wirr-wirr dunlin

twit grey phalarope

twite twite

twitik yellowhammer

twitterwitter swallow

twitt-itt-itt goldfinch

twit-wit knot

tyik-tyik sanderling

tyit red-necked phalarope

tystie tystie black guillemot

tzee spotted flycatcher

tzeeip hawfinch

tzee-tsee-di-ree-zzurrit shore lark

tzee-tzee-choor-r-r crested tit

tzee-tzucc spotted flycatcher

tzik hawfinch

tzitzi grey wagtail

tzueet siskin

tzwik Savi's warbler

uk-uk-uk great black-backed gull

ung-unk bean goose

urrah cormorant, gannet

urrah-rah-rah-rah-rah gannet

urrrrrrr Savi's warbler

urrurrurrurr nightjar

vit vit-vit-vit swallow

vuvuvuvuvuvuvu snipe

wah-onk Canada goose

wait middle spotted woodpecker

wee-chew peregrine

wee chirri-tew-ee-o tew-ee-o tsee wir-ri-o ir-ri-o robin

weecho-weecho-weecho coal tit

weee-wee-wee red kite

wee-it purple sandpiper

wee-jee jee-jee wizz did-ju-ee did-ju-ee redstart

weeka-weeka-weeka black-tailed godwit

week-week-week pomarine skua

weela-weeo golden oriole

wee-o golden eagle

wee-oo sparrowhawk

weeoo red kite

wee-ou woodlark

weep mallard

weest rock pipit

weet-a-weet green sandpiper

weet-chack wheatear

weet tweet weet-weet green sandpiper

wee-tuc-tuc spotted flycatcher

weet weet wit-wit-wit whitethroat

wet-we-wit quail

wha-wha-wha cuckoo

wheat-whit purple sandpiper

whee pintail

whee-oo wigeon

wheet chaffinch, meadow pipit, redstart, sedge warbler

wheet-tsack-tsack-tsack stonechat

whet-whet garden warbler

whit grey phalarope, pied flycatcher, red-necked phalarope, tawny pipit

whit-tew hen harrier

whit whit sanderling

whit-whit-whit red-necked phalarope

whitz water rail

whoop-whoop whooper swan

whushee black grouse

wibwibwib pochard

wick great grey shrike

wicka-wicka black-tailed godwit

wink-wink pink-footed goose

wit-e-wee dotterel

wit wit little grebe

wit-wit green sandpiper

wot-wot dunlin

wow-wow-wow cuckoo

wrreee kestrel

yaaarr Slavonian grebe

yah arctic skua

ya-wow arctic skua

yek-ek-ek Montagu's harrier

yew pomarine skua

yowk-owk-owk great black-backed gull

zee-chi pied flycatcher

zeeda-zeeda-zeeda-sissi-peeso goldcrest

zeee zeee goldeneye

zee-it zee-it pied flycatcher

zeep corn bunting

zee zee zee coal tit, crested tit

zee-zee-zee grey wagtail, long-tailed tit

zee-zee-zee-zee goldcrest

zeezeezeezeezeezia firecrest

ze-ut meadow pipit

zeu-zeu-zeu-trrull ortolan bunting

zhree waxwing

zink zink great tit

zirlrl cirl bunting

zir-r-r-r waxwing

zit cirl bunting, Dartford warbler, firecrest

zi-zi-zi goldcrest, willow tit

zree treecreeper

zwee greenfinch

zzee-at goldeneye

17. Sometimes a bird will forget part of its repertoire.

18. Calls vary in number and complexity from one species to another, and from one individual to another.

Mnemonics

Mnemonics for bird sounds are listed separately, as they are formulated in a different way. The "bird words" of the main lexicon attempt true phonetic equivalents of the sounds birds make, whereas mnemonics catch the rhythm and emphasis of the song in words and phrases from the English language, regardless of the failure of vowel or, especially, consonant sounds to equate. One particular mnemonic takes this detachment one stage further: rather than supply the rhythm of the song, the phrase for the chaffinch describes an event whose own rhythm suggests the song.

This selection is not intended to be, and cannot be, a comprehensive guide, as there are countless local variations and birdwatchers often make up their own. As a rule phrases only are listed here; single-word mnemonics (such as ca-ro-li-na) are regarded as phonetics that happen to coincide with existing words, and appear in the main listing.

North America

are you awake? me too   great horned owl

bob white, bob white   northern bobwhite

but-I-DO-love-you   eastern meadowlark

cheerily, cheer-up, cheerily   American robin

come here, Jimmy, quickly   solitary vireo

cover it up   brown thrasher

de-ar-ie come here yellow-throated vireo

don't you dare yellow-headed blackbird

drink your teeee rufous-sided towhee

drop it, drop it, pick it up, pick it up brown thrasher

fire, fire, where, where, here, here indigo bunting

here, here, come right here, dear Baltimore oriole

here I am and where are you? red-eyed vireo

hip-hip-hurrah king rail

I am so la-zee black-throated blue warbler

listen to my evening sing-ing-ing-ing vesper sparrow

maids, maids, maids, put on your tea, kettle, kettle, kettle
song sparrow

oh dear me golden-crowned sparrow

one, two, three, four, six magnolia warbler

O sweet Canada, Canada, Canada white-throated sparrow

please please pleased to meetcha chestnut-sided warbler

poor Sam Peabody, Peabody, Peabody white-throated
sparrow

purity purity purity bluebird

qu'est-ce qu'il dit? qu'est-ce qu'il dit? . . . great kiskadee

quick, three beers olive-sided flycatcher

spit and see if I care, spit! white-eyed vireo

spring of the year eastern meadowlark

sweet, sweet, sweet, I'm so sweet yellow warbler

take, take, take it easy Savannah sparrow

teakettle teakettle teakettle Carolina wren

three-eight yellow-throated vireo

trees, trees, murmuring trees black-throated green warbler

what cheer cardinal grosbeak

when I see you I will squeeze you warbling vireo

which way sir? Maryland yellowthroat

who cooks for you white-winged dove

who cooks for you, who cooks for you all barred owl

why don'tcha come to me? here I am right near you hermit
thrush

Great Britain

a little bit of bread and no cheese yellowhammer

cheerily, cheerily, be we glad robin

cricketer running to wicket, bowling chaffinch

go back, go back, go back back back red grouse

may the devil take you yellowhammer

take TWO cows taffy wood pigeon

teacher, teacher great tit

tree, tree, tree, once more I come to thee pied flycatcher

wet my lips quail

whither I flee, whither o whither I flee skylark

19. One bird will never repeat another's song exactly.

20. Some sounds are classified more consistently than others.

23. No attempt to standardize notation of birdsong has ever succeeded.

24. Attempts to convey the voice of a bird by means of written language must necessarily lack precision.

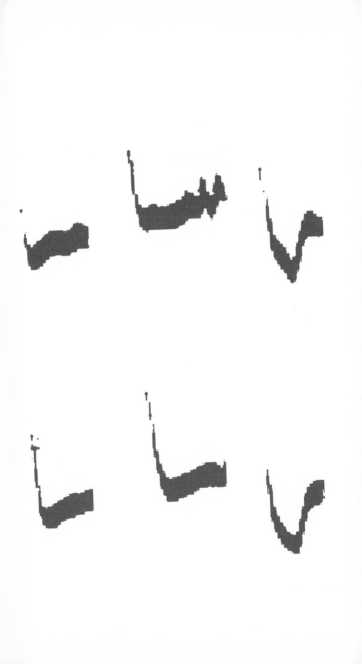

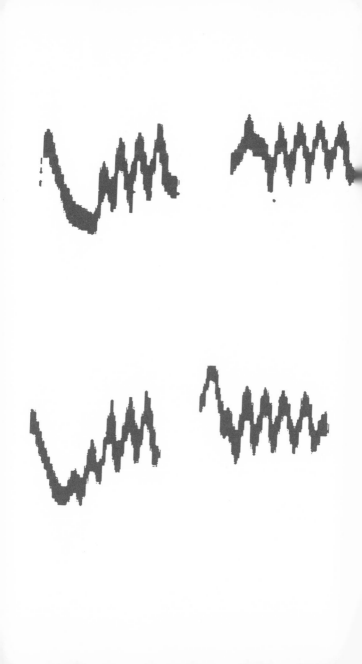